Cover design by: Gregory Cain

CONTENTS

COMFORT KILLZZZ

If you choose to believe that sleep is the cousin of death, then accept the fact that comfort is that long-distance cousin sittin' by the cooler at the summer cookout. Best believe that comfort has its sunglasses and a coy grin on its face while lounging in the corner scheming on who is next. Comfort, although we seek it and do all that we can to get our hands on it, can actually do more harm, more damage than we can anticipate. If you remember nothing else, take this thought away - "comfort killzzz".

COMFORT KILLZZZ
INCORPORATED 2023

CHAPTER 1 - COMFORT KILLZZZZ

I believe that comfort is the kin to sleep and that sleep is the cousin of death. Killzzz is spelled with three z's to emphasize this belief. Our comfort can put us to sleep or better stated, comfort positions us to no longer be awake although alive and well. That is, no longer 24/7 placing the same effort into reaching that next goal. Being consumed by our purpose, or for some, the next goal, is not a bad thing. Striving and reaching for the momentary comfort and satisfaction that comes with reaching the goal is great. Hoping to hold on to that comfort forever is where our problems begin. If we aren't careful, the immediate comfort can lull us away from our purpose in life.

This thing that we call life is filled with layers. Things we can control vs. those that we cannot. We create, build and develop in order to make life better. We also deal with the ramification from things life presents in which we cannot control. In all that we do, we make efforts to make life livable or comfortable. This comfort that we seek and work hard for seemingly is the goal and basis for our activities and actions. With that said, I ask you to ponder the thought - what happens when we reach our comfort zones? Although the concept sounds great, Is this what we REALLY want out of life?

Think back throughout the history of civilization. What comforts did our ancestors forgo so that we can live as we can do today? Lewis and Clark chose to leave their comfortable homes and families to explore the western portion of the United States. I don't know about you, yet dealing with the Rocky Mountains, the arid land we now call the Southwest region and many challenges they faced on the expedition does not sound too comfortable to me. Great benefits have been realized due to the comfort being sacrificed for the purpose of exploration.

I have great respect for our soldiers and military families. How many wars and battles among nations have transpired over time in efforts to make life better for future generations? Great immediate comfort was sacrificed in order to free groups of people from tyranny, oppression, depression and for many other reasons.

What if life's comfort for these men and women were greater than the desire to perform these and many other heroic actions? Wouldn't life today and the historical record of our existence be drastically different if comfort was the priority for those in these roles? Hmmm...

As we look at this concept historically, let's take a look at it relative to our lives today.

Comfort can be defined as a "state of physical ease and freedom from constraint" or "the easing of a person's feelings of grief or distress". Using this as a working definition, it is possible to see these elements in our lives today.

As a society, we have shown in many ways the things that we are willing to do to obtain comforts or to enjoy the ease of life:

- How many wars have been fought in the name of freedom from rules and control?
- The number of Inventions to make life easier
- How many laws have been passed, debated and broken for comfort's sake

I challenge the theory that comfort should be the goal as I believe that our comfort is one of the limiting factors to our greatness. I know, I know, my point sounds counterintuitive. Allow me to express this via a few examples:

Comforts we seek can actually serve as kryptonite did to Superman. We can get the zzz's, the itis if you will, as a result of comfort. We find ourselves drained, less determined, sleepy and lazy relative to our purpose, ambition, and our time.

Comfort can kill our purpose. Our purpose is the reason for which something is done or created or for which something exists. Those reasons to do or to create something can be minimized once our comfort takes over. Fulfilling our purpose can seem hard or too big of a challenge when most of the things that we want or need are in reach. At times, it is easier to do the things we can do versus the things we should do, those things in which we are purposed to do.

Comfort kills our ambition, our strong will to do or to achieve something requiring determination and hard work. The effort and determination required to achieve greatness has to be greater than our current level of comfort. It is more likely that our ambition takes time, along with our strong will. I'd like for you to consider that our comfort shifts by the hour, by the second at times. If our bellies are empty or if our pockets are light, may be the factors that impact our ambition. I ask that you take the long term approach. Work with your ambition, your strong will; let's not allow our comfort to drive us away from our goals in life. Your desire to be great should outweigh your desire to be comfortable.

Comfort killzzz our schedule especially when we make efforts to have the comforts of life to fill our calendar. Why replace the beach getaway, because of our available time and current cash levels, with service to ourselves and others. Too much hard work, right? Terrible example, I am sure, yet the point is that our human nature makes it a challenge to do less with our comfort in order to do more with our heads and hands to make life better for ourselves and others. Reading two books to be a better professional or to be a better person could be less enthusing than scrolling through social media or adding items to your favorite store's shopping cart. The trade-off most likely occurs down the line when we wish that we prepared ourselves more for what is ahead than resting on our laurels when comfort is on our side. Let's allow some comfort to remain in our schedules, yet I ask that you also make time to do what you are here to do. Get it done....

Comfort can wipe out our gifts and our talents. I hope this startles you just a bit. That thing that we do so well can become a lost art when not used. Certainly, the gift, the talent doesn't "go away", although it can seem that way when we do not tap into it or use the gift with some sort of frequency or relevance. Using what we have been given positions you for far better results than using what we've accumulated or purchased over the years. Use what you have been given, this day, this opportunity, this hour to be the best you can be.

When you have all that you need, desire and place in contention, why would you then fight, scratch and claw? What reasons would you have to dive into the fire, give your best effort, sacrifice and the like? Wouldn't your comfort prevent you from doing all the above? Let me try it this way - why would you come down off the mountaintop to solve the problems of those in the valley? Maybe it is just me....

When you are in the valley, striving to make it to the mountaintop, comfort is not on our minds. Our minds are filled with trying to find the way out, to make enough magic to get that perceived place of comfort, the mountaintop. I'll ask the question again, if you make it, why would you come back to the valley to fight the same fight?

Comfort kills our ability to dream

If you would agree, our existence is due to the dreams of our ancestors. The thoughts "what if" or "can I" or "maybe if we could only..." led to trial and error then eventually success. That energy and effort to find a new way can be challenged by our comfort. Maybe I am the terrible one in the room for being honest. I will not have the need to find new methods to make life better - I have all that I need. I'm comfortable. Exaggerated point, yet comfort is not our friend

Comfort kills our resources

Time

Money

Capacity for greatness

Comfort can destroy our legacy

Harder to continue to accomplish

Less desirable to develop and build when we are relishing in comfort

Comfort kills our ability to prepare & perform

Why do the routine and boring steps to prepare

I've made it..

What is the need to stay sharp? I got it all...

Comfort kills our desire to press forward, shift & adjust

Life will continue to put more and more on our plate

Living in that place of comfort makes us less nimble and willing to shift

Many of us deal with frustration, fatigue, lack of desire, lack of grind and more as we navigate life. It is not always due to your diet, lack of exercise or not consuming your vitamins. I ask that you consider if your comfort is the reason that you are not where you'd like to be. I will openly admit, my comfort has cost me dearly. I hope that you noticed that past tense - historically it has cost me. I've "made up my mind" that I will use what I've been given each and every day to help others. That decision has worked wonders for me. I encourage you to make a similar decision for yourself. Although I am not in the "answers" business, I have thoughts, ideas, and recommendations for your consideration.

Give yourself the litmus test - based on your efforts to reach your comfort zone, how well has that worked out? Keep your answers to yourself....

CHAPTER 2 - NEW ERA, NEW STATISTICS

Yesteryear is dead...The sooner that we recognize that we live in a new era, our life gets better - immediately! Yes, instantly. We have to also recognize that new statistics are here as well. The measurements of progress and success change over time. For those of us that are 'creatures of habit', we have some work to do.

How many of us cringe at the sights and sounds of our new society? We scratch our heads, sometimes out of disbelief, sometimes we are just bewildered and amazed. We are forced to come to grips with the fact that life, as we've known it, as we recall, just isn't the same. You or someone you know may be challenged by the 'scoreboard of life'. The wins versus the losses - the failed effort vs "it is the thought that counts" concept - the answers to the "how well did it work out" questions. Here is the magic for someone today. Right or wrong, we must take time to come to terms with the fact that in this new era, new statistics tell the story. It is not my point to convince you today that these new statistical categories are sensible, right, good or just. My only point today is to remind you that they exist and that others indeed use these new statistics as a form of measurement of progress and/or success. I'm not debating right or wrong, I just want to clearly reiterate that new metrics exist in this new era.

Allow me to paint the picture this way...Could you imagine measuring your net worth today by the amount of gold or livestock you owned? Laughable today, yet that was the case at one point in time in our society. Having eight or more children so that you could effectively take care of the farm, ranch, share-cropped land or plantation? Sounds ancient, right? Just a generation or two ago, that was the measuring rod. These statistics may appear to have shock value to some, yet these were applicable measuring tools of life historically.

Any Major League Baseball fans out there? Anyone remember the days of determining the best player by their batting average, hits, homeruns, RBI? Good statistics in these categories historically landed good players huge contracts and signing bonuses. Sorry to inform you, that a professional sport with well over 100 years in existence has completely changed how it tracks, measures and records progress and success. Can you feel me driving this point home?

Taking it one step further, the word statistics is rarely used anymore, the terms sabermetrics or data analytics is in play now. A good professional baseball player is determined by the following among many others:

- **WAR** - Wins above Replacement
- **DRS** - Defensive Runs Saved
- **SoR** - Strikeout % Rate

It's not my job to explain these baseball statistics in great detail. It is my job to emphasize the fact that these new measurements are here. Not only in this sport, yet in life.

I'm sure the baseball reference wasn't all that fitting for all. Allow me to try another example. I am here to remind you that your favorite rapper, singer or entertainer has different metrics as well. Historically, how many times have you heard stories about going gold or platinum following an album release? How many times have you heard about the opening weekend ticket sales for the latest blockbuster movie?

Although those statistics are active and maintain some relevance, they are no longer the primary statistics for planning purposes or decisions to be made. The promotional plans are based on views, impressions, influencers and advertiser responses. I know...so different, right? New era...new statistics.

Cash isn't king anymore! Historically, how many times have we been advised to keep some cash on hand. You remember, in case of a toll road, inoperable ATM machines or if you get "stuck on the side of the road". It made so much sense, didn't it?

The technology-driven card readers may not work, they may not have power or wi-fi, carry some cash - was the sentiment, right? Ladies and gentlemen, we are now trending towards cashless venues. Yes - that is correct - cashless. Paper currency or our coins are useless in these locations
Talk about a new era! Some of us thought we'd never see a day in which cash is no good. I'm just trying to paint this picture, new era - new statistics

We have shifted as a society. Your life, my life, just isn't the same as it used to be, statistically speaking. I am not advising you that you have to change immediately how you measure your progress and success in life. I am telling you that the shift has occurred. You are an adult, use the perspective on life that serves you best. That said, let us not lose time or miss opportunities by acting like this societal shift hasn't occurred. We know that our historical measurement methods are just that - historical.

I encourage you to not be afraid to shift as well. Shifting does not mean that we have to change who we are or what we are at our core. It may mean that we change how we see ourselves. Possibly update how we operate / how we move, modify our behavior and habits to shift how we measure our progress and success in life. The world evolves - so should we. Yesterday is gone...

CHAPTER 3 - ALL CHANGE AIN'T THE SAME...

How we see the world can impact our ability to survive & thrive. How we see ourselves plays an important role. How we view others and scenarios playing out is equally important. In this chapter, my aim is to emphasize this point. It is all about **CHANGE**. Here are a few questions to deliver in your mirror.

How do I deal with the ever-evolving aspect of life?

How do I process change?
do I actively run away to avoid it?
OR do I boss-up to then run towards it?

SEEING LIFE CHANGES
We recognize change so much easier in others, don't we? Much easier in others than in ourselves for many of us. Have you had any one of these conversations?

Are you going to the gym or changed your diet?
It looks like you've lost a few pounds

Wow - your baby is walking now?
It seems as if they were just crawling yesterday?

He is a Freshman in high school now?

"Wow, I can remember when he was in 3rd grade"...smh

This may seem or sound fairly routine as others are involved in those questions. Well, what about changes in your life, in your circumstances? At times we have to remind ourselves as adults that we are no longer 21 or 25 years old, right? That first day back in the gym when you thought you would merely shoot a few hoops...

That first day back in the classroom after 20 or more years away...

That time you thought a quick jog was a good idea...

“I thought I could hop back in, like riding a bicycle”

“I didn’t know it would take me this long to recover...”

“I didn’t know I could be sore for 5 days after that”

If any sound familiar, think about the fact that change in life is so subtle. We tell ourselves that we used to be able to do all with no problem, then we find ourselves asking one of the questions listed above. This is my point today, in life, we often treat days, hours, relationships, work as if it has always been the case, that we can do things exactly as we’ve done before. These experiences teach us to recognize that change is apparent - it’s real. It reminds us that we must accept change or that we will be forced to deal with it.

EXAMPLES OF CHANGE FORCED UPON US

In life, we will have seasons in which we have no control, no input or influence on what or when changes will occur. A few examples:

- **Birth** - crawling, walking, talking while fully reliant on others to survive and to grow

- **Youth** - transition from full reliance on others to independence

- ❖ **Manhood / Womanhood** - establish who/what we are in life in adulthood; our beliefs

- ❖ **Cycles of Marriage / Birth** - witness new additions to your life; your circle; your family

- ❖ **Ailments / Aging** - changes in how we live, walk, talk, navigate, prepare, perform

- ❖ **Death** - we witness / observe others depart from this life as we await our date

Relationships change as well. It doesn't always matter that you've made changes or if you resist change. Some happen without our input. Relationships cycle through seasons as life does. From day to day, they cannot remain the same as the days and years pass. Kinda just how it works...

That said, it is my opinion that the best relationships are the ones in which we modify the rules of engagement as the circumstances of the relationship changes. Many of us will anticipate the relationship with a loved one or co-worker to remain as it was established. Rarely is that the case.

Expect and anticipate relationships to shift over time. It is not possible for the terms to remain unchanged over time. We are doomed for life to "beat us up" if we expect anything else. Communication about change and how we feel about change - is essential. Knowing where we stand positions us to adjust accordingly. Whether we adjust in a timely manner - if at all, is another story.

At some point in life, the follower becomes the leader. For example, Dad may teach son the family business. As the son watches, listens and learns, change occurs and the roles reverse. Yes, even in parenting, we see change play out. The caretaker must be taken care of at some point.

As we attempt to manage change that occurs in all ways, shapes and forms in life, a combination of strategy may be utilized. Some life scenarios require us to think/make decisions, others force us to adapt and overcome, whereas others, we have to hang in and hang on until the next season arrives.

Make every effort to remain confident as you face changes in your life. The changes that you can control. As well as those changes in which your two cents matters not, practice agility to adjust accordingly. Believe that you can endure and thrive following any circumstance that presents itself to you in life.

PREPARE for the only constant we are promised in life - change. Get excited about the changes that are coming your way. Grind throughout all circumstances as you stand and deliver your best.

Remain confident in your beliefs and your ability as you demonstrate your skill in managing change.

CHAPTER 4 - WE ALL GET THE SAME 24...

Consciously or subconsciously, we often attempt to shape or mold the perspective of others. Think about how we treat political issues. If you watch a news headline scroll across your television screen or your social media feed, then go watch a progressive news outlet followed by the conservative outlet. It is possible to wonder if the same topic is being discussed. Two completely different perspectives, right? I encourage you to know who you are as those winds can blow you all around if you allow.

Ever witnessed a conversation between someone who is extremely religious with someone who is not religious at all? Rarely is the conversation about the matter at hand, often each party has to defend their perspective - 'til the end - right or wrong. Sometimes, the issue at hand becomes secondary to each party drawing that line in the sand.

Even at the end of a school year. It is summertime for the kids. Some view this as a reward, a break from a long school year. Others, potentially some parents of school-aged children, see summer break differently. Solutions and decisions have to be made regarding child care, camp & workshop fees, daily transportation, three whole meals per day and I have to listen to them all day? Albeit comically stated, that perspective can be overwhelming for some.

Those scenarios lead me to the topic for this chapter "We ALL get the same 24...". Those 24 hours that we are given are precious. We vary greatly in how we use those hours each day in life
It is easy for some of us to wonder:

- "How did they achieve so much?"
- "When do they have time to rest or even THINK?

On the flip side, some may ponder:

- What do they do for a living?
- I always see them on the porch or at the house...
- Do they ever leave?
- Do they work?

In essence, we may wonder what others do with their time, what they do to earn their money and more. Take note that it is not cool to count other people's time or pockets. Let's not do that today or any day for that matter. Returning to our topic - We all have the same 24...yes, the time granted each day.

How do your view your 24? What is your perspective on time? Is time a gift or a curse? Do you SPEND time or do you PASS time? Think about that for a few moments.

The time spenders anticipate a result out of their currency. In this case, we are talking about time, not money. The time passers seem to hope that time just flies by in front of their face with no attachment, no goals, no living or enjoyment of life in the forecast

We can squeeze quite a bit into those 24, if our perspective positions us to do so. I hope to influence someone that is seeking a new point of view, a new way of viewing those hours that cycle day into night. It is okay if you are seeking or are willing to consider new thoughts and new ideas on how to make the most of this thing we call life. I'm not in the "answers" business, yet I'd like to share some ideas with you today.

Make an effort to focus or or to strengthen your belief system - whatever it is that you believe in.
This can add value to your life, ability to handle joys and pleasure, while serving as that rock to hold onto when the days are tough.

Can we use some of our 24 in preparation? Could we improve individually by considering preparation during our 24? What are we preparing for?

- Prepare for that next job, relocation to that new city
- Prepare for the unknown or the unexpected
- Prepare our minds and bodies for the days to come

Take time to think / reflect. This concept may sound too simple for some. However, taking time to reflect on things that have gone well or not so well provides a chance to review our choices and show gratitude for our chances - the opportunities presented to us daily.
Reflection can help us sharpen our tools. Thinking will help improve your preparation skills. That said, overthinking can paralyze us as we analyze our failures, flaws and mistakes to no end. Although it is quite important to reflect, overthinking eats at our capacity to:

- Press onward
- Prepare for the next season
- Enjoying the days that we have been **GIVEN**
- It is a dream killa', too!
- I can't be a winner with those mistakes
- Overthinking life can put us on the sidelines
- Process your thoughts, let 'em go

Time, those 24 hours each day, is a gift. None of us did anything to earn this day. I petition you, plead with you, to make the most of what we've been given. Allow me to remind you, that we may not be gifted with these 24 tomorrow. Let us remain thankful for the chances that we are given. Let's remain thankful for the choices that we are allowed to make each day. Use your precious 24 each day on your business (business of life). Although we serve others, lend a helping hand to assist in times of need, do not give away any of your precious 24 on other's business. Focus and you and yours - We all get the same 24 - use them wisely!

New rule: Master your priorities, not time

Focus on what you need to do; not the hands on the clock. Some of us go to work thinking that we have 8 hours to do 5 things. I'd like to influence you today to rephrase that sentiment. You have 5 things to do with 8 hours available, earmarked if you will, to do that and much more! I ask that you choose to view time as an opportunity. Use each and every opportunity given to benefit #1 (YOU), to use your gifts and talents and to serve others.

Believe that you can make the most out of what you've been given...Yes, that includes that 24 hours that you have in each day.

CHAPTER 5 - GAMBLE ON YOUR #1

I am certain that many of you have heard the phrase, "What happens in the dark will come to the light"? I challenge that thought as I attempt to encourage and motivate you. What if there is a chance that what happened in the dark remains right there - in the dark. Hmmmm....

Somebody is wondering about skeletons in the closet, about salacious activity from the past, those days or moments we wish we could have back for a do-over. Worry not - that isn't the goal. My aim is actually just the opposite. Think of those things that we worry about coming to the surface, the things done or said to hold you back, the phases of your life where fear and doubt made light work of you. The times that you limited you and your greatness, that yolk that should have broken your neck and back years ago - those things.

Guess what, **you** and **only you** have those things fresh in mind. That is the point of this topic. Some of those items haven't nor ever will, come to life. You remember, you may have scars, you may even still feel shame or remorse. Please know that yet your next boss, your next employee, your next problem solved has no clue! It simply doesn't matter. I ask that you live as if it will remain in the dark forever bringing forth the lessons learned to help others to get better. Take time to unlearn your failures, flaws and missteps that have held you back. Keep all of it in the dark.

Some of us may have failed at something 20-30 years ago. Some of us had a teacher to tell us that we would never amount to anything. Somebody reading had a bad educational experience in high school that they still think about in the 40s or 50s.

We, the world, do not have that same recollection. Please stop operating as if a sticky note remains on your forehead of that failure or misstep. We don't know anything about it. We, the world, don't care! That is the encouraging word for someone - we don't care about your mistake in 1997. We don't know that you were not at your best, your 100%, back in 2013.

Get off the sidelines - stop hiding from that failure in which we know nothing of. I know when you were in your 20s, you moved outta momma's house too fast and they reminded you of such. They scared you to death with the fussin' and long speeches, right? That was decades ago, those missteps way back when cannot and should not hold you back today. We can be so afraid of letting someone down that you are afraid to move or to keep it movin'. That misstep stays in the dark; it won't bite you today. That pain of shame, it hurts. It has made you better because of it. It is my opinion that your Middle School teacher that didn't believe in you **cannot** be the reason that you remain on the sidelines today. It just can't.

I say that sarcastically because I know how easy it is to allow that pain of yesteryear to hold us back. I repeat - it cannot or it should not be the reason that we remain on the sidelines today. Protecting yourself from shame in which we, the world, knows nothing of, cares nothing about is fruitless. Although your concern and pain is **real**, I ask that you make every effort to put it in your past so that you can keep on movin'. You've got work to do, gifts and talents to use, problems to solve! Allow that pain to stay in the dark, yet I ask that you come out of that dark place so that

GREGORY CAIN

you can be great!

GREGORY CAIN - THE COMFORT ZONE KILLA

We all can use a bit of help to shift or improve how we see ourselves and how we operate in life. I believe that we must break our comfort zones to learn new things as we develop personally and professionally.

The Comfort Zone Killa' is here to help you to break your comfort zone.

- Give The Comfort Zone Killa' a chance
  Consider the opportunities to improve
    - Personally
    - Professionally
    - Relationships
    - Maximizing your gifts and talents
    - Focus on your #1 - YOU
    - Achieve the goals, dreams and aspirations you were placed here for
- Focus on the four cornerstones
  - **Belief** - hold onto it when life gets hard
  - **Confidence** - keep in ample supply - keeps fear & doubt at bay
  - **Preparation** - get ready; be ready; stay ready
  - **Performance** - get into the game; execute; make magic happen

I can help you via learning sessions, training or personalized coaching. Let's discuss what works best for you, your team or organization.

COMFORT KILLZZZ INCORPORATED

Comfort Killzzz is an educational nonprofit 501c3 organization focused on improving communities where citizens are capitalizing on their gifts, talents, resources and opportunities available to them by breaking their comfort zone, increasing skill and confidence levels through learning or training opportunities. This organization intends on serving the community by hosting and facilitating learning sessions in the realms of:

- ❖ Professional Development
- ❖ Personal Development
- ❖ Small Business Development
- ❖ Technology Skill Development
- ❖ Job / Career Improvement

The mission of Comfort Killzzz Incorporated and the Comfort Zone Killa', Gregory Cain, are to further personal & professional skill development, employability and confidence within the community via technology, small business development, career development and financial literacy training.

I ASK THAT YOU...

- Believe that you can
- Believe that you will
- Maintain your confidence
- As you prepare to perform using all that you've been given

Comfort Kills, Incorporated 501c3
educational nonprofit organization
www.thecomfortzonekilla.com
info@thecomfortzonekilla.com

www.ingramcontent.com/pod-product-compliance
Lightning Source LLC
LaVergne TN
LVHW050612100826
845148LV00015B/3230

* 9 7 9 8 2 1 8 2 2 1 5 3 9 *